Tiny Team Park Leaves a Mighty Big Mark

A book about young activists

Written by,
Rachel Albert, Sarah Park & Team Park

Illustrated by,
Rachel Albert

White House photo, AP Images/Patrick Semansky
Special thanks to J. Potash for permimssion to use images of posters

To the kids I work with at school and to the kids I am raising at home- YOU inspire me. Keep leaving your mark to make the world a better place.

R.A.

Because of Mie Devers- for showing me there is always light around the bend.

Because of Team Park- for giving me far more than I could ever give. You inspire me to always keep learning. You all are absolute treasures. Absolute treasures.

S.P.

In the year 2020 the world felt upside down. There were opinions in the air, there were tensions in the air, and there were germs swirling in the air, too.

1st grade in Ms. Park's class was fun and friendly. It was special and sincere. It was meaningful and memorable. Still, it was anything but normal.

The Tiny Team Park scholars were all at home! COVID-19 had closed school buildings, and Team Park could only share connections across their computer screens.

The COVID-19 pandemic wasn't the only thing that made this year different. There was also a presidential election. The last time there was a presidential election, Team Park kiddos were only 2 years old! Now they were learning about real issues in their world and in their community.

Their teacher, Ms. Park, saw them as activists. Every day, they shared their ideas to spread kindness. Even though their bodies were small, their ideas were so, so big.

Team Park had ideas to change the world!

After the election, they looked at activists' signs on and near the White House fence. They read the words, they interpreted the symbols and they responded to the art.

Some signs reminded Team Park of their classroom essential agreements, reminding them every day how to treat each other to make the world a safe place for everyone.

So much of the action was happening on TV and on the news. Washington, D.C. seemed so far away and Team Park wanted to make a difference.

Should they try to go to the big city?

Should they wait until they are grown ups so that they can vote?

That feels so far away from now!

Sometimes grown-ups show kindness to others by cooking good food, but kids can't always do that by themselves.

Sometimes grown-ups drive places to tell someone something important, but kids don't know how to drive.
What could Team Park do to share what is on their minds?

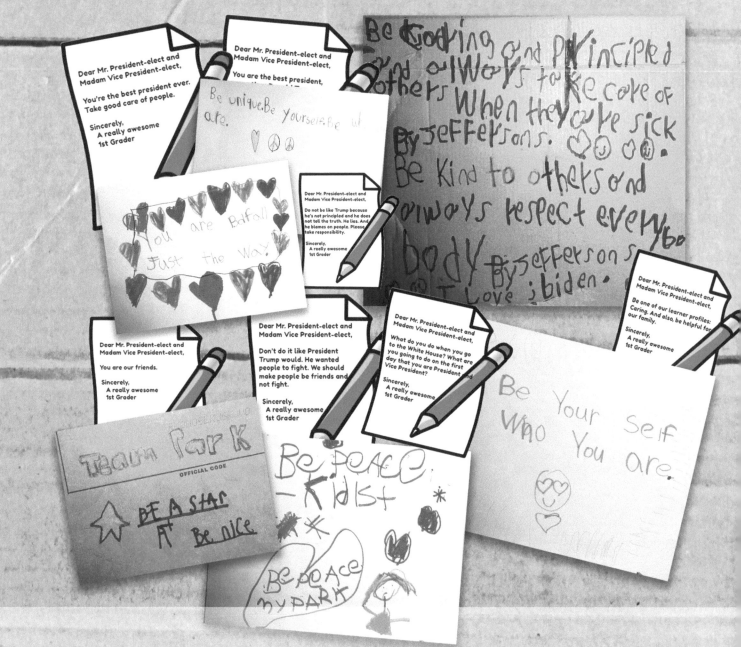

Ms. Park asked her tiny scholars to write letters. She asked them to make signs. She asked them to make their voices heard.

Ms. Park, along with her friends from school, took
Team Park's signs, art and messages directly to
the White House.
They put them on the fence
for everyone to see.

*Photos of visitors stopping to look at the messages that Team Park shared with the world.

What messages of kindness would you want the world to see?

These little leaders were putting their hearts out there. They were learning that their voice matters. They can be activists for kindness and justice. They know the power of love and they are the leaders of our future.

What sign would you add to the
White House fence?

What do you want elected leaders to hear
from your heart?

Make **YOUR** voice heard!

Send your signs and letters here:

For letters to U.S. Senators:

Office of Senator (Name)

United States Senate

Washington, D.C. 20510

For letters to Senate Committees:

(Name of Committee)

United States Senate

Washington, D.C. 20510

https://www.senate.gov/senators/contact

President and Vice President of the United States

1600 Pennsylvania Avenue NW

Washington, DC

20500

Note to teachers and educators:

When was the moment in which you found your voice? Perhaps it was a singular and powerful moment that catapulted you into your voice-consciousness, or perhaps it was a series of little moments gathered together. What if our young children, humans, leaders, and scholars could experience that moment-- that moment of voice-consciousness and realizing you've got to lift your voice for the things that matter-- in their earliest years? What kind of world would that create? How would that transform our world? Reflecting on these questions will always propel me towards hope. As teacher educators, or anyone who is creating space for children in any capacity, we hold immense power. We hold immense power in creating spaces in which the vision of community holds another immense power to color a young human's ideas and expectations of equity, responsibility, and community for the years to come. How do we wield and share that power responsibly? Our youngest humans are engaging their eyes and ears, seeing and hearing and listening and feeling. They are absorbing the world around them, whether we are aware of it or not, whether we would like them to or not. How can we be responsible for the impact that we have? Austin Channing Brown says, "I believe that to practice love is to disrupt the status quo which is masquerading as peace." How can we make way to practice a new kind of love, a deeper more expansive kind of love, a radical love? I believe it starts with ourselves, and accepting our role as truth tellers. As Cornelius Minor likes to say, I am radically pro-kid, and "that means that it is our job to create opportunities for children and eventually we teach children how to create opportunities for themselves. As such, anything that stands in the way of opportunity for a child is my enemy. So police shooting brown children... you can't read if you're dead. Kids being malnourished because they live in food deserts... you can't write powerful poetry if you don't have all your vitamins. And so these issues, they're teacher issues." It's also critically important to balance the truth of injustice with the truth of beauty, to continually amplify joy and humanity. This work is hard and it is challenging... and it is so worth it.

Note to parents and caregivers:

Raising kids in this world is challenging. We want our children to be aware of the world around them but that world is often filled with dark and disturbing images. Our kids hear of protests and riots and vigils all too regularly. We want to teach our kids about varied experiences and perspectives and yet we still sometimes need to shield them from reality. Reconciling the degree to which we expose kids to the news and also how to impart the importance of standing up for those less fortunate or for issues that align with your family values is complicated. I suggest starting with positive messages and actions. Teach your kids to stand **up** for what they believe. Send letters of encouragement, hopes and dreams. When your kids become older activists, they'll be able to find plenty of reasons to attend protests and riots to fight against injustices. While children are younger, take them to parades, marches of solidarity and community gatherings. Martin Luther King, Jr. said 'Our lives begin to end the day we become silent about things that matter." Talk to your kids about standing up for what matters. Talk to them about the importance of leaving their mark, in a peaceful way, so that world can hear their voice.

CPSIA information can be obtained
at www.ICGtesting.com
Printed in the USA
LVHW070622180621
690564LV00021B/1516